# RETURN

# TO

# INNOCENCE

# CRAIG A HUBER

# RETURN
# to
# INNOCENCE

# Craig A. Huber

Kravitz & Sons

INNOVATORS IN PUBLISHING, MARKETING AND ADVERTISING

Kravitz and Sons LLC
204 E Arlington Blvd. Suite B
Greenville, NC 27858

Published by Kravitz and Sons LLC.

ISBN:  979-8-89639-607-9 (sc)
ISBN:  979-8-89639-606-2 (e)

Library of Congress Control Number: In Progress

# TABLE OF CONTENTS

Acknowledgments ............................................................i

Innocence...................................................................... ii

Regrets ........................................................................ iii

Chapter 1 : Darkness.....................................................1

Deceit ...........................................................................2

Hailstorm......................................................................3

Wireless.........................................................................4

Hidden...........................................................................5

Nefarious.......................................................................6

Craziness .......................................................................7

Arrogance ......................................................................8

Corporate.......................................................................9

Entrapment..................................................................10

Barren ..........................................................................11

Faithless .......................................................................12

Abyss............................................................................13

Evil...............................................................................14

Danger .........................................................................15

Chapter 2 : Look Inside...............................................17

Redemption .................................................................18

Attacks .........................................................................20

Seeking Holiness .........................................................21

Enlighten .....................................................................22

The Drive Within ........................................................23

Boldness.......................................................................24

Rise Above ...................................................................25

Keep Moving................................................................27

Collection of Love Poems ............................................28

Over the Years ............................................28

Purity ............................................29

My Mate ............................................30

Arrival ............................................31

A Flame ............................................32

Enduring ............................................33

Timeless ............................................34

Silent Whispers ............................................35

Quiet Embraces ............................................36

Maggie ............................................37

At Last ............................................38

Finding Home ............................................39

Finding the Light ............................................41

Searching ............................................42

Restless ............................................43

In Touch ............................................44

Revival ............................................45

Cleansing ............................................46

Empowerment ............................................47

Patience ............................................48

Freedom ............................................50

The Golfer ............................................51

End of The Day ............................................53

About the Author ............................................55

# ACKNOWLEDGMENTS

Sarah and Crane, my parents
Linda, my soul mate
Harold Funston, my golfing buddy
Joe Grover, Wooster School English Teacher
Dana Shaw, an understanding mentor
Rob Womack, a great friend and consultant
Holly and Austin Mee, Editorial consultants

# INNOCENCE

Ever miss the days
When you could run effortlessly
Making a fingertip catch
Sliding on your chest
In the mud
Or on a sled
Against a deserted hill
On a wintry eve
Lit by a faint light
On an old wooden pole
Innocent to the deceptions
That betrayed our hearts

# REGRETS

Looking into the eyes
Of my youth
Contemplating where
I am to what I might have been

Crossroads appeared
So indiscriminately like
Waves upon the shore
While seagulls scream
Piercing confidences

Indiscretions left
A hollowing soul
Mired in a tortuous abyss,
Only now in prayer
A cleansing gateway to peace

# CHAPTER1:DARKNESS

Sin comes into our lives unconsciously
And pride can take us so low
We lose touch with our aspirations, and maybe our souls
Born of fear, anger and abiding loneliness

# DECEIT

Imprudent chattering
Sardonic impressions
Encompassing the airways
A calamitous source

Grey film sears my brow
Distorts absolutes
Once fortified
By virtuous intents

A roller coaster rumbles
East to west precariously
On old wooden tracks weathered
By repertoires of unscrupulous tack

# HAILSTORM

Words omnipresent
From multiple devices,
A whirlwind of hail
Swirls without remorse

Aimless tweets
Penetrate solidarity
Startling a deer at rest
Desecrating humility

Big words intertwined
With multiple spins
Masking control of free will
And evil desires within

# WIRELESS

The heart cloistered
Paralyzed by the speed of light
Exasperating the mind,
The technology maize

Digital space, seemingly innocuous
Brilliant genius, intelligent bliss
Thought without a soul, prevalent
Masking veritable intentions

Connections without presence
Lifeless and isolated
Repelling effervescence
Fostering loneliness and despair

# HIDDEN

The tongue and the pen
Instruments of power
Eloquent and precise
Belying the weakness of souls

Demoralizing innocence
Truth and honor,
Courage left unattended
On bar stools chattering and gazing

Dreams shattered
Caught in a web of conceit
Petrified of failure
Though already defeated

Like gutless buzzards
Gouging the prey of their scorn,
Finding solace communally
Heartless and perennially barren

# NEFARIOUS

As cunning as a serpent's con
Calculable words and transparent eloquence
Propagate instant gratification,
A dark cloud covers the sun

The devil's playground
Enticing thoughts, seep unbridled
Bolstering arrogance
A peacock's haughty array

The heart, the generator of hope
Smothered in tears of despair
The eagle, our proud protector
Looks down forlorn, withered and endangered

# CRAZINESS

Grey walls trapping
Street people begging
Bureaucrats scheming
Politicians edging
News people shading
Cameras invading
Talk hosts chattering
Half-truths surrounding
Idols evolving
Self-worth dissolving
Evil pervading
Sensitivities decaying
Hope flickering
Tears piercing
Memories protecting
Faith beginning

# ARROGANCE

A desperate guy
Touches but does not feel,
Frowns but does not laugh
Cool and serene

Who sees both sides now
His little boy tossed aside
Flexing his marks
Avoiding self-truth
Rationalizing his actions

Impervious to honor
Sarcasm reigns humor
With the best hit,
A lucky night,
A forgotten conquest,
Stone cold With stoic conceit

# CORPORATE

Gossips, rumors
Seep insidiously
Around barren desks
Cluttered with remnants
Of salad bars so stale,
Waiting for weeks end
To be a spectator of fun,
A prefabricated soul,
Trapped by the
Bureaucrats grasp,
A playground of
Thankless smiles
Permeating a cold chill
Behind your back
A lifeless blight,
Escaping to the
Solidarity of a
Computer's stare

# ENTRAPMENT

Entrenched in staunch opinion
And secretive intentions,
Communication non-transparent
Outwitting the innocent of heart

Yet weeds grow unabated
Cracking seemingly impenetrable concrete
Revealing incalculable guile
Only to recede inauspiciously

Alliances come and go
Like a spinning wheel
Casting fate to interim advancements,
A repertoire of spiritless strategies

# BARREN

Naked loneliness
Dancing for green
Dirtied by wanting stares
Of hardened passion,
Misguided truths,
Love left behind

Swirl on to the next look
Ill conceived hope
That weakens the heart,
Wearied the soul
Around and around,
A touch without a kiss
Ungratified to the
Pounding of bronze waves
Overbearing rivers
Unkempt by industrial green

Face the desert
With stern decor
Look back to the sleet of ages,
The lustrous snare,
To bury the pain
Into a cemetery forgotten
From which aspiration
Arises above the
Lilies in the fields.

# FAITHLESS

Witches in the dark
Laughing at fortunes so slim
Preying upon insecurities
Of troubled times,
Under the guise of spirituality
With reference to the universe
Not cognizant of God

Enamoring pieces of your life
Revealing a destiny so clear
Overwhelmed with such clairvoyance
Your relief is short lived
An investment so bare
Ill fated trust deceived

# ABYSS

A winter solstice
The sanctity of solitude
Succumbing to ubiquitous loneliness
Propagated by an incessant March howl

Unforgiving transgressions
Devoid of grace
Emaciated, clinging spuriously
Emboldened by marketing fantasies

Sanctimonious collusions
Beguiles humility
Expunging initiative
Drifting in mazes of self-deceit

# EVIL

Permeates souls so subtle
As the sharpness of a scalpel
Poisons the heart

Abhor the admission of
Slurs seeping from your tongue
Piercing honor, integrity, and stature
Left to the repercussions of insecurities

# DANGER

A temporal flash
Electrifies a foreboding haze
A coral snake slithers cunningly

As roguish tongues disparage
The nobility of souls,
Chilling and deplete

A culture once principled,
Now desolate and crestfallen
And oblivious to an impending storm

# CHAPTER 2: LOOK INSIDE

Staring at a timeless surf
And salt laden foam,
A source of perennial strength
Nurturing beyond the
The chattering of seagulls
Meandering aimlessly
Between thundering waves

# REDEMPTION

Ever wonder why feeling so incomplete
With fear destroying dreams
Surrounded by veils of mendacity
Momentarily rid by fantasies
Conceived in your mind
Without the guidance of your spirit
Bolstered by beer, wine or worse
Fortified by gossips and late-night excursions
All fading as the tide goes out

Imagine yourself
A dancer on the stage
A poet on the beach
A gladiator in grasp of victory
As you search someone
To listen to what you project to be,
Fooled by their intentions
To fulfill their gaps too

Where is your hero within
Lost in bad habits
Of dreams passed by,
By lack of commitment
Of unforeseen tragedies,
So unexplainable,
Where is hope
Why the uncontrollable pain
Remaining desolate

From the depths of nothingness
Broken on your knees
Courage simmers slightly
The hatching of a deceptive shell,
Persistence replaces pride, anger subsides
Nevermore will tragedy or success evade
Your quest for happiness
Love of you, of God,
The real battle begins

# ATTACKS

An ache awakens
Within the chest
Ominous and pervasive

Circles of distractions
Rushing an array of arrows
From an enemy unseen

An evil force
Manifests anger, masks deception
Attacking peace

Then, the silence of rain
Soothes the soul
Cleansing the mind

Raindrops build upon
A green bedrock
Around folded hands

The smell of blue hews
Eastern herbs and gardens
Calm the restlessness of sleepless nights

# SEEKINGHOLINESS

Capricious winds billowing
Inducing desperate thoughts
Oppressing sanctity
Caught in webs of deceit

Mendacity goes unabated
Behind a moray's devilish smile,
Incessant gossiping permeates
A forlorn metamorphosis

Upon my knees searching
As there is no way to go
Amid a crisis of malcontent
Recovering to a holy state

# ENLIGHTEN

In the darkness of my thoughts
Dangling on a cliff
Precipitately within my soul
Grasping for short term conquests

Passions roam aimlessly
Frenetic responses
Conditioned by past digressions
A frayed existence

A penetrating light
Inspired by a renewed mind
Forges new horizons
Leading to unconditional love

# THE DRIVE WITHIN

Ever watch the persistence of ants
Never abated by stinging rains
Rebuilding instinctively
Their washed-out abodes

Dark clouds knocks upon our souls
Incessantly, permeating our hearts
Our spirits downtrodden, hanging
On the precipice of despair

An array of paths
Slip behind our minds
Blinding discernment to God's touch,
Deliver yourself from fallen ashes And
Breathe deep in stubborn resolve

# BOLDNESS

I'm a boxer
In the ring Tenuous at first,
Shunning shudders
Of bad habits ingrained,
Taking a bold step
To the power within
Like chasing salmon
Upstream,
Eroding a demonic gap

In the twilight
Of my life
I begin again,
A violin pierces
My heart as
Soft humility
Wears away Tears of the past
To be the best me,
Innocence anew

# RISE ABOVE

Dreams of youth
Radiate a freedom
Of being, while
Insecurities creep in
Behind walls of canard
Life moves swiftly on
Solitude becomes bliss

We are all artists
Sparked by a Flickering
To seek transcendence,
Like a motionless stream,
Surreal, reawakening
An ubiquitous force
Towards destiny

Flourishing with
The gentle blossoming
Of a rose to the moodiness
Of a summer rain,
Burning ashes wither under
The pureness of white snow,
A passing to our rebirth,
Creativity reformed

Artists make images
Suppressing the compulsion
To control one's being.
The livelihood of their joy

Capture this truth, or
Die in self-made prisons,
Abound in search
And live uncomplicated
Within the intricate balance
Of nature's grand design

# KEEP MOVING

An evening run,
A morning's walk
The rustling of
A reticent stream
In a fly fisher's thoughts,
The exhilaration
Of a sudden catch,
A skier's last traverse
Burning the thighs
High over the last jump,
A golfer hitting a
Drive effortlessly,
The touch of a
Putt feeling the grain,
To the sound of a crisp
Chip against an
Azalea mood,
The runner in us all
Raising one's arms
Kissing the sky,
The joy of exertion
Breaking the chains
Of self-doubt,
Building a spirit of
Endurance so pure

# Collection of Love Poems

# over the Years

# PURITY

Listening to your dreams
As you drift into my arms
So warm and tender,
Like a soft breeze
Blowing sparkles off the sea
Reflecting the multitude of stars
Emitting Rays Of eternal love,
Brightening the dawn Of our journey together

# MY MATE

What would happen if
I gave you my heart
When overwhelmed by roguish darts,
Invisible and deceptive

And the silence of snow
Confounded by a world depraved,
Dissipating into a forlorn mist
Suppressing a celestial peace

And then your caress, assured
A crystal of precious light
Unravels snares of tentative thoughts
My friend, my rock, an eternal gem

# ARRIVAL

There were times
When traveling the road
Was more of a purpose
Than the destination reached

The loneliness of the trip
Endured many heartaches
And thoughtless stares
Across darkened bars

While the lack of fulfillment
Of the place arrived
Made the road Seem so inviting

Until I met you
Without effort
And now, the road
And the destination are one

# A FLAME

Like a crack
From burning wood
You entered my life
Unspoiled passions
Slowly rise within me
As my power unfolds
Into the best man I can be

You are there
As pristine as
A doe gazing,
Your soul molds into mine
With intentions pure
Listening to the breezes
Seep through the willow tree

# ENDURING

She entered from
Behind my heart
As if she was always there

Quiet strength
Warms my soul
A mate unwavering

As trials attack
The passion of dreams
Slipping towards temptations

Belying trust
Causing sleepless nights
And worrisome visions
Dissipate as the morning dew
Settles on the sanctity of our nest
Held loosely by fragile straw
Fortified by enduring love

# TIMELESS

Remembrances
Of withered trails
Traversed before time
Alone in wonderment

Your radiance opens
A new passage
Forgiving wayward indiscretions
Cast upon aged canyons

At the end of the day
I await the rapture
Of your touch
An intimate embrace

# SILENT WHISPERS

Soft breezes, the silent lapping
Of tender ripples against
The bows of ships, cutting
Through a myriad of moods
Understanding without words

Blinking fog lights, so distant
So close to the pounding of waves,
Upon rocks projecting
God's touch: Dreams, ideas, creation as
Rainbows calm troubled seas
To the security of your smile

The end and beginning of a week
Times of peace,
The quest for new horizons
Begins again,
As your head lays on my chest
Another moment with you

# QUIET EMBRACES

I touch your mind, you feel my heart
I hold your hand, you read my eyes
I caress your hair, you hear my thoughts
I bring you close, you see my dreams
I shed a tear, you uncover my strength

I lift you up, you sense my pain
I offer you silence, you know my purpose
I gaze into your eyes, you already knew
I try to explain, you only just smile

I am humbled by you, you grab my arm
I am lost for words, you are at peace
I am on my knees, you kiss my brow
I am here, you are no longer there
You touch my mind, I become your heart

# MAGGIE

She would look up
Mischievous and affectionate,
Touching the innermost portals
Of my heart, unconditional

Stubborn and resilient
A salesman and an entrepreneur
Advocating walks in the park
Constantly sniffing the variances of life

Nonjudgmental
As God intends love to be,
Innocent and loyal
A perfect blend

And as the passing
Of the ages seep indiscreetly,
Her head lays against my arm
Licking an undying tear from my face

# AT LAST

The lightness of your heart
Falls gently as
A feather
Upon my hands,
Humbly restrained
By the reverence
Of your touch

Tossing you
Upwards,
A dove of white
Tapered to a
Clear blue sky
In wonderment
Of our new flight

My arms become
Wings of hope,
Searching together,
Silhouetted by the sun,
Releasing many clouds,
An enchanting journey,
The ultimate fulfillment
Of our life

# FINDING HOME

A train drifts
Alone on a timeless path
Guided by a circular light
That reflects on silver tracks
Along a river from a
Source unknown,
Passing towns and cities

Traversing another crossroad,
It leads out from sorbet dust
Through yellow waves of wheat
And aspen leaves to
Norwegian snow
Blue gazed from northern lights
Eternal fjords to
English gardens,
Perfectly squared

Day and night
The rumbling goes on
Through thunderous storms
And eerie howls,
To discover the river's birth
My homeland complete
My mate secured
No longer passengers on
Trains that never cease
Another port, an endless destination

For an instant,
Or a lifetime,
My heart blends

Imminently,
Only distracted
By forlorn whistles
In the dark, remembrances
Of travails painted away
By the stars of my dreams

# Finding the Light

# SEARCHING

A river stirs
My restless heart
As soft snow
Ushers solitude

Frequent whispers
Sanguine and assure,
Flow unabashed
Enduring memories

The tide recedes serenely
As a forlorn beacon searches
An omniscient eclipse,
An incessant quest

# RESTLESS

Whispers in the night
Spinning out of control,
The rustling of sheets
The darkness of thoughts
The devil's delight
A despondent blight

Pervasive and persistent
The night is an eternity
A spirit going awry,
Tainted dreams
Mischievous fantasies
Festering mendacity

Upon my knees
A peaceful recluse
Before the rise
Of a morning fog,
And then a wisp
Ignites the sun within

# IN TOUCH

A drop of dew
A mist immersed
To the slow beat
Of a fog horn,
A boat creeping

In the mountains
Solitude
Listening to the
Crack of a limb,
A deer breathing

The late sun
Dissipates
Into a morning scent
A brisk wind
Arrives on an afternoon shore,
A red sky at dusk
The sea now a glass lake

Warm rain
Falls across my cheeks
Upon my knees
In earnest prayer,
The forgiveness
Of his touch
Comforts my heart
An eternal bond,
Everlasting

# REVIVAL

A light sun
Dries an encumbering mist,
Revealing
An untainted image
Of what was once
But now only a distant blur

Plastic surgeries
Nor a cherished liquor
Can camoulage the distress
Of a lailing heart,
A listless soul
Lost in a self-made maize

Look beyond the crude
The nothingness and despair,
Breathe in a crisp fall day
Before the leaves lose
Their splendor and grace,
With bereavement comes life

# CLEANSING

Walking through the waves
Of my tears dripping
Upon a forlorn heart

The music of my youth
Conjures honorable images,
Impervious to underlying schemes
By the stillness of a river's edge

A perennial cracks crusted soil
Seeking the recluse of holy grace
Pondering the mysteries of it all
While serenity caresses my inquisitive soul

# EMPOWERMENT

Traversing the ages
Of my past
Through my mind

Grasping for vintages
Encased in my soul,
Unforgettable memories

Seem so distant, surreal
Grasping for a shred
Upon which conidences reside

Like a caterpillar dredges
To her cocoon, unwrapping
In yellow brilliance

Flying so free,
Arriving in harmony
As God intended to be

# PATIENCE

Wait, when the pain persists
Hold your hands in the fold,
Break the chains of those clinging
Demons, leaches and the unforgiving,
The dreams from your heart
Must survive the plagues
From the air below the sun

Wait, when lying awake,
Alone with tears of past sins
Hurting from unforeseen hits
Like sharp waves
Beyond understanding
Testing the fabric of the soul

Wait, know the path is lucid
As a crystal with many beams
Shooting forth your potential
Searching under the strain
Of the last grasp,
Cramped legs
Staying balanced
While running free
In the valley of darkness

Wait, happiness is eternal
Your lessons learned
Your destiny understood,
Captured as subtly
As the falling leaves
From the ginkgo tree

Wait, for dreams
Are the stuff to strive
Within the portals of hallowed halls,
Princesses, Princes, Queens and Kings
All appear as one
Awakened by a kiss
Of a running stream

# FREEDOM

Tentacles of sin
Attack from fear unfounded,
I crept under a facade
Of my own choosing,
Illusions unkempt,
Fortified by fantasies,
All emanating from my mind
Painted by dragons and justifications

Walk away to innocence
Days of painting daisies,
Walking the dog,
Shooting hoops in the street
Laying in the hay,
Staring at whispering clouds
Mustering the courage
To never surrender
To the demons around

I choose my own path
From the guidance above
In the solitude of thought,
Running a deserted shore
Beyond the noise from crowds
And indiscriminate stares
Of urban sprawls,
The pain of past indiscretions
Melt away to the light
Of a blameless day

# THE GOLFER

A wisp arises from
A familiar cigarette,
Preceding the flight
Of his balata rising
Against a maroon sky
Catapulted from
A swing of beauty

Analyzing mechanics
He drifts into his zone
Hearing a drop of dew
A determined focus
Initiates perfection momentarily,
A gift from above
Surviving the ages
With uncommon grace

His game an art
His passion untiring
Chasing a golfer's dream
An eternal quest,
To walk the green carpet
Of Azalea fame
Seeking the perfect round
To God's delight

And as the ashes
Fall aimlessly upon
The final hole
Amidst crickets chattering
And the sweet smell of heather,
His putt drops gently
Defying the evening dew

His smile pervading
Another day, another dance
My buddy Harold had game
Always has, always will,
A mentor to all
That transcends the game

# END OF THE DAY

Gazing down a barren track
An orb appears in the distance,
Stretching out from the womb
Grasping for a warm embrace

Boarding my designated train
Hesitant and alone
Greeted by many passengers
Through the passages of life

Traversing to the caboose
My vintage journey unknown
The chattering relentless,
A chill freezes my spine

Comforted by laurels
Tempered by regrets,
Vigilantly straining for incandescence
Beyond a foreboding horizon

Upon my knees
Arriving upon a mystical cloud
A harmonizing union, feathered
By God's majestic touch

# ABOUT THE AUTHOR

*Return to Innocence* is Craig's second poetry book. He is a devoted husband and has two wonderful children in Ashley and Craig Jr. and 9 grandkids in Luke, Maybelle, Madelaine, Wesleigh, Ollie, Wren, Atticus, Laeken and Elowyn. He is a graduate of Wooster School, Springield College, and Columbia University. He was a former member of the United States Olympic Committee and helped found the sports association for Cerebral Palsy Athletes. He has had a variety of professional experiences including a current position in advertising sales and being an avid golfer. Poetry is a hobby for him in writing about evil, love, forgiveness, and faith in God.

www.ingramcontent.com/pod-product-compliance
Lightning Source LLC
Chambersburg PA
CBHW031235120626
46545CB00003B/1133